POPPY

✦

AUSTIN HUMMELL

POPPY

✦

AUSTIN HUMMELL

— Del Sol Press • Washington, D.C. —

DEL SOL PRESS, WASHINGTON, D.C.

Paper ISBN: 0-9748229-2-2

FIRST EDITION

COVER IMAGE: *A Boy with His Final Dinosaur,* Drypoint Etching,
    Robert Shetterly

COVER & INTERIOR DESIGN BY ANDER MONSON

The text is set in Fournier 12/15.

Publication by Del Sol Press / Web del Sol Association, a not-for-profit corporation under section 501 (c) (3) of the United States Internal Revenue Code.

CONTENTS

I

II

III

IV

V

ACKNOWLEDGMENTS

The following poems have appeared in the following magazines
and anthologies:

Controlled Burn, "Long Blond and Gone," "It Was a Kitchen to
　　Live In"
Chalimade Literary Review, "Charlie Chan," "Columbo"
DIAGRAM, "God's Early Church," "Alien Abduction," "The
　　Desertion of Nouns"
Fugue, "Obsession for Ocelots"
Gettysburg Review, "Helen's Cordial," "El Niño"
Gulf Coast, "Kaspar Hauser"
Hiram Poetry Review, "Heroin," "Equus"
Like Thunder: Poets Respond to Violence in America, "Panic"
the minnesota review, "In the Great Green Room"
Melic Review, "I'm Not Up So Much As You Are Down"
Poetry, "Sunday Morning Percodan"
Pinyon, "Galleons Lap"
SHADE, "Butterfly Ballot," "Royal Street Jug Band"
The Southeast Review, "Jackdaw Shade"
Terminus, "The Professor and Mary Ann"
32 Poems, "Giants," "Dr. Emeritus Speaks at the Department
　　Meeting"
The Wisconsin Review, "Panic"

for Alisa

O my God, what am I
That these late mouths should cry open
In a forest of frost, in a dawn of cornflowers.

— Sylvia Plath

— I —

GOD'S EARLY CHURCH

Whole months pass without sun. February
all coffee and the stink of iron. Once,
a girl from Carolina left me
for dead. Something about ambition
and the ropy vein in the bend of my arm.
I lanced them both with flowers from another
country. You should have seen it.

Years of that until the windows were full
of a juice called methadone designed I guess
to sweep the streets of me. I weighed myself down
with coats of it. I unplugged the voices of my friends.
The world? Fuck. I can't get enough of it.

SUNDAY MORNING PERCODAN

There are days when a big wind kills her son
calling long distance from Uz, Oregon
and even the sunny throne of coffee
won't do. Days when the pressure of heaven
drops the barometer and her ankles
talk back to the clouds. Already the old wound
of a rib has knit from scarring
but not her marriage, so she tips
too many pills from the orange light
of a bottle whose script has blurred.
She spoons cream in her coffee
twice a day, shrugs once every four
hours, takes God as needed, and prefers
love before it expires. In an hour
the world will freshen and a new church
will press its spire through the ruth
of her heart. The rumble of her husband
will turn back to words she wants,
the cats will own her lap, she will lunge
the stairs in half and answer each question
the phone asks. What is faith
if not this, this opiate reaching its
tiny hands into the lobes of euphoria,
this hymn that dips or psalm that lifts
her eyes, this heart like the swollen
heart of Christ astride a donkey,
with the lazy palms of Sunday waving hey.

LONG BLOND AND GONE

No more of her hair to pull from the drain,
from winter flannel or the pillow case,

from the collar of coats that didn't fit;
no way to know when you draw from your lips

a thread of false blond in a web tangle
of saliva—when at the tip of the tongue

a tickled trick of nerves leaves a phantom
trace of her you sputter, not out of pride,

but from that need most of our cavities hide
to empty themselves, to rest unfathomed—

no way to know if it is even hers
and not cotton fever, some junkie blur

of a weekend when you fumbled enough
of an oath to leave a taste in your mouth.

HELEN'S CORDIAL

She came in vinaigrette from the bedroom
with a syringe raised like a distaff of gold
flax, like she was the mother of exiles
explaining the cloudless harbor of New York.

Came because she had seen them freeze before
when they tied dope to a drunk. Seen the sleep
in the dying face, the rigor in the arms and neck,
the mouth like the stem of a breathless raft.

She knew the bluing lips and blanching face,
the body ferried too far, the eyes like coins.
She knew it was hers, the stuff still uncut
by baby laxative and speed, that took him.

So we walked him like a chair to his car—
our arms crossed beneath him in a throne
we summoned from childhood and weddings—
and left him for the sirens to swallow.

She said sometimes flowers are more than flowers
and Greek the language of gentlest sleep.
She came from the bedroom like Helen came
in Sparta, both motive and heroine,

to drown an old war in her husband, free
the gall of his friends. Came to us smiling
with a needle she said we'd share. Told us
how he scarred his arms and roped his hair

and wore the paper clothes of the homeless,
and when he walked down into the birdless
air west of Atlanta, how they took him in
with the gentle, deadly love of junkies.

OBSESSION FOR OCELOTS

*Dallas Zoo researchers, looking for ways to save
the ocelot by encouraging the endangered cats to
breed, have found a scent that drives them wild—
Calvin Klein's Obsession for Men.* (CNN)

It was a rut made of musk
and a lucky guess, when some novice
at the Dallas Zoo splashed CK
onto the backs of the disappearing cats.

I guess it was too much to live caged
with the scent of rainforest fading,
to be fed by buckets and clocks,
the rounds of trout stripping the vim

from pursuit, the mordancy from hunger.
Face it. The sex we call animal is lost
on them—the itch for leather, the rush
of handcuffs, the mouth's many transgressions

and the drunken love of strangers.
But today they track the cologne
that draws every sex of eighth grade
through the glossy pages of heroin chic,

the same scent that draws a bulimic waist
to the oily face of a boy
tying a belt around his biceps,
the scent that tells us desire

is beyond our control but a cage
worth paying for, that what we want,
really want, is blond, starving,
and bored to extinction.

THE DESERTION OF NOUNS

First to go are the names of fruit
and the people you haven't loved.
The dental assistant who pats your shoulder
when the drill stops, the waitress whose smile
was broken by stroke, the mailman
with his tattoos and tramp of snow
in the late morning. Call him Karl,
Karl who you've seen in the produce aisle
talking to himself because he can't remember
if it's turnip or mustard greens
that the man he has loved for twenty one years
wants, the man he talks about on your porch
with uninterruptible speed but whose name
escapes you now like his illness, though you
recall its manifestation in spots,
in the gentling of memory. Spots
like the ones blooming beneath the tan
on your hands that you notice when
you take your uncle his omelet. For him
there is nothing so lucid as 10 am,
when the spills of breakfast settle
and a nephew returns with a tray of nouns
and a name just below his forehead.
Starts with a B. Even in the snarl of tissue
we call his brain you count one hundred
trillion synapses down which chemicals
still whip fibers and tear across cell divides—
one hundred trillion to lay down the jumpy tracks
of memory, nudge his blood, chill
what is left of terror, schedule sleep,
help him walk or shape a plan
to kill himself. *Bird*, he says, *Ethel Merman,*
with rope. The day I rubbed my friends
from the Memorial Wall. Pomegranate.

PANIC

In the night woods, any stir is sudden—
A syrinx fallen to leaves, the shuffle
of a goat's foot, the sound of your own voice

startling the silence a capella.
Even kids own the awe of a god there,
ruminant in cover, redolent of sweat.

So we named a new fear in the forest,
half for a wanton god, half for the sightless
alarm it caused us, flaming like contagion.

We pressed our backs into the pillowed terror
of children asleep beneath the Black Forest,
of the cruel pruning of a daughter's limbs, and waited

for the grim click of light switches and closing doors.
Now we try to forget—when halfway through life
the swirl of blue lights and sirens shocks us

to the icy shoulder of an alien road,
when the plane we're in dips and pivots
in a pocket of wind, when the phone at 3 am

flushes sweat into the cradle of our palm—
that the woods are still alive, deserted

by parents, that no forest is so black
as the one we wake to, children still.

— II —

THE ISLAND OF MISFIT TOYS

Somehow you lasted through the shame
of wrong colors, past a blonding
jaundice, a nose ruddied by birth,
past an eye pinker than a shell's belly.

Still you cheer the blue-black genius
of the crow who beats his head
on an attic fan to salute his boredom.
Even the complacent laces

of your son beneath a spruce
islanded by sheets and tinsel
thrill you, slowed though he is
by an extra chromosome.

He has loved an ape with one eye,
painted whiskers on his pretty pug face.
He knows the three things you need
to starch the night of a fawn. An icepick,

a dentist, and a jack-in-the-box
named Charlie. Could be that island
in the life of a child made timid
by difference is full of soot and toys.

IN THE GREAT GREEN ROOM

Think how our voices slow and octaves fall
when we read to the sleepy, how lazily
we grope for the page when it runs out of words,
how we pinch off its corner as if rubbing
granules of salt into a soup we haven't yet
decided to trust. How the turning stalls
the sport of cows, the sleep of bears, and our faith
in rhyme as it leaps, slantwise, from room to moon.

Night wants a rhythm slowed by pages as much
as a lamp does, but the lamp wants a book open
to the grin of a mouse. The hands, they prefer
the symmetry of mittens stiffened by fire.
The mind understands the need to goodnight
a room made alive by a child's fancy,
a world a window barely frames, stars and all.

In the legend of paint, green is a secondary color,
like the room after the room your mother
burped you into. Pitch is what swallows light,
and the baby girl panting into a monitor
is who swallows her mother most of all.
Goodnight saddlecar, goodnight milk. Good riddance
to hats and beef jerky and shoes. Goodnight mail
and tissue and hair. Goodnight things the room has
to tear. Goodnight dumplings and thumbs and mirror
and god. Goodnight my ma, my face, my oh.
Goodnight yellow bird. Goodnight no.

GALLEONS LAP

If we can name the place between autumn
and death, between the worn elastic of muscle
or socks and the gently rocking harp
an angel troubles like the surface
of a clouded lake, then call the distance we drop
from monkey bars to first grade
by its own name, something like
Horse Latitudes or Galleons Lap,
something to say how hard we thrashed
or how easy the sailing, what we kept
and what we drown.

Once it was enough to soothe a donkey's
melancholy, to squat cross legged
in a circle of sixty trees to quell
a bear's fluster. Once it was enough
to wish sticks down a stream.

It was never an easy logic, not
like the cut and dried syllogism
of a father with a belt looped
in his fist. Not the soft logic of dreams
either, but more the conceit of a schooner
with too many decks, or that spot
we went to talk where the ugh in thought
got lost, that place we learn to disenchant
with Latin, as if childhood were the bother.

GIANTS

They never learn from tripping
over the shoelaces we tie when they nap.
The love of giants is clumsy and dear

for this. In the middle of the night
they call to nobody with their hands cupped.
They just never learn from tripping

sailors the risk of wine. Even in friendship
they drop their hearts like melon, blind to betrayal.
The love of giants is dear, but clumsy.

Like most people they are wary of beans,
fond of gold, and do not eat the British.
It's just that they never learn from falling

that people like them better when they're dead.
At times they lumber back to us, drunk, but not always
is the love of giants so clumsy. Dearly

they stoop to kiss and hear us, tongueless
and smiling as the mothers we run from.
The love of giants is clumsy and dear.
They never learn, refuse to learn, from falling.

MIRROR MIRROR

You were slow to learn the queen's trick
to bully it until it wakes
in agreement with you. The day
puberty silvered your face, bats
nested in the disobedience
of your hair. July whitened you.
Snow framed your every blemish.
There was the boy who bent his flower
over the puddle of your eyes.
Too often the heart that you held
in your hands was a pig's heart.

It's not hunger, now, that shrinks you
to a voice in a cave thin as echo.
In café bathrooms you turn to it
holding your breath, batting your eyes,
giving back daiquiris and salad
before you digest them. As for the lake
about to claim you, you coax it
like the queen in Snow White until
a wake silvers the last of you,
or what you've always seen in such
glass—too much, too much.

EQUUS

The kid with the nose ring says he thinks
it's about horses and when he says horses
his lips tremble because his tongue pierce
didn't take. His teacher says what about sex
and he says no but thanks and she says no
I mean the poem and he says no hawses
and his lips bounce again as he reaches
back for the r and since they won't purse
like the lipstick kisses of great aunts
he sounds only numbly British
though regal beyond his parents' income.

He's thinner than her daughter, most daughters,
because his mother let him eat anything
and he didn't. When nightmare came
he'd slink down the marble stairs on which
his father, spavined by gin and mad
with quarrel, once shattered his speaking
and a porcelain Morgan. In the kitchen
he'd graze the apples as if stroking something
small or cold as a pet's nose, open an ice box
someone named Bronco and pull sugar cubes
or chocolate milk from the jungle of olives
and Frappuccinos his mother calls a diet.
Nights he'd stand there and speak tenderly
to cheese, coo the name of condiments
by breed, and when he shut night's loneliest light
he'd leave in the jaws of the box
more words than his mother ever wanted.

Still she says what about the tongue stud
and he pretends to misunderstand her again
so she says no I mean why did you put a stud
in your tongue and she says it like she's speaking
underwater or Malaysian for the first time
but he knows what she wants so he nods
and when he smiles back his lips he says
it's the last place his parents would look.

KNOTTED TONGUE

He tried every word with nervous consonance
as a child. When tetherball stuck in his mouth
like gum or Wonderbread, he chewed it sweating
till it came. He ducked the plosive, preyed
on paraphrase, thrashed at synonyms
and faked a thoughtful brow in the spasm
of each hesitation.

               He loved any answer that was six
or yes, all questions that settled for a head
shake or gesture of hand. But he loved best
the guessers with rich diction and prescient
hearts, the ones who knew all the czars
and box scores, who memorized his foods
and sitcoms, and patient, read him like braille.

When a stammer puppets his face,
cinches his mouth like a leather purse,
when a hard c tourniquets his chest and stones
his lips, he give thanks to these: the gorgeous muteness
of sports, the shushes of movies and music,
and the riddle of fluent whispering,
when all his prayers are lucid
as the second breath of Moses.

KASPAR HAUSER

I cried and said horse, horse,
because my feet hurt so much

　　　　　　　—Kaspar Hauser (1812-1833)

Or consider the wordless, like the foundling
boy who rises from a hole in the German
earth in his sixteenth year knee-less
as a cheap doll and gropes toward Nuremburg,
a wad of ribbon and a blanched and sanded
toy horse in each hand.
　　　　　　　　　　For the first time
he witnesses the difference between day and night,
his arms crossed to guard his eyes from the sun.
Every one he meets he meets for the first time,
but just to speak is to groan or weep
apology, to whisper *Ross*, the word for horse
the man who locked him up dropped in his ear.

When horse is the obliteration of the world,
he begs for a hole where horse means longing
for a horse, or thank you for this ribbon.
Horse is both the music from a peasant's wedding
and the laughter, horse the sadness
of a lame boy too weak or scared to carry
a toy over the threshold of a foster home,
horse the pain of all walking, walking an awkward
compromise between falling down and standing up,
horse the last word he whispers before the pain
of talking faints him to sleep. Horse is even
that last shadow lunging, horse the dagger
that cleaves his heart like a plaything, like a child's
hand, like the pearled neck of an Arabian,
Kaspar thinks, bleeding to death. Something to stroke,
something to dress, something to call by a favorite name.

— III —

LAVENDER

Kim Novak's a really good faker.
She falls in love with your hands
first, then falls like a sack of meal

from a church tower. Just for you.
Since it is not her breath, the wind
frightens her, and neither is the water

below the golden gate quite the ice
of her goodbye. If the blond eddy
of rivers dizzies you, she washes her hair

like laundry and swirls it in a bun.
She's like the girl grades above you
once who dozed in social studies

and woke in a relief map
of India. The girl whose family
you could never find in her face.

No father bent over spectacles
or an engine block. No mother
to summon with a squint's wish.

She was the first dream of a girl
whose dream was never you.
How you candled your avenues

till she came. The thought-lost milk
of her hellos, the lavender skirt
she washed in the foam of breakers

once. It killed you then like Kim Novak
kills you still to know that any guy
could dress her, change her name,

break her for sport. In the shallows
she'd have been a perfect blue,
if not for the smile, the trace of blood.

THE PROFESSOR AND MARY ANN

On her the smile of a rag doll readies
for flattery or purpose because corn
is her origin, corn her choice,
as if she split the life of a woman
and traded the hips and breathy sex
of an actress for cutoffs, a tablecloth
halter top, and a name rustic as Norma
Jean. And he is nameless, a guy in white
with eyes like a microscope
and his face flush to the lens of escape,
too distracted or dumb to fall swinish
to the spell of a pout or hair like flame.

In his dream he mends the radio diodes,
irrigates beach sand, jars a new species
of *Thorybes Confusis*, and repairs the Minnow
with the gum of an undiscovered phylum
of mammalian plant. And when they gather
in Sweden, those of science and judgment,
he will have charted the uncharted desert isle,
and the world will know his name.

In her dream she is Ginger,
glitter flaring its gown at her fullness
as she walks the voodoo island walk.
In her dream the howl of millions rises,
the jaw of the skipper drops, the jungle eyes
of the first mate bulge into monkeyhood,
and the mind of whitest science
drops its squint from the small crisis
of extinction and follows her as dawn
wells into the lagoon's mouth.

COLUMBO

The word rosebud reaching through the phone
to Dobermans; the digitalis beneath
his bicuspid crown; the careless way
you stubbed his cigarettes. Almost always
the smallest mistake, like the dental record
in the apple you bit at the crime scene,
or the unwitting flick of the light switch
after staging a suicide. All that hard work
left hanging in the double-crossing dark.

And just as you begin to curse your father's
nags about the cost of lighting daylight
he turns to you, this dumpy gumshoe
bent like a courtier under a London
Fog , a cigar wedged in the barrel of fingers
he taps on his temple—and asks another question.
Begs, really, like his dog Dog, stroking your pride
with sad-eyed reliance and knitted brow.
Your job is always better than his job.
Your celebrity is known even to his wife.

But by the end of the day your steps are small
and difficult, your wrists are braceleted
and kiss at the pulse, and when the press
in all its flashy attention clamors
for you, whatever your celebrity
was, you are famous all over again.

ROYAL STREET JUG BAND

The wind down Toulouse loosens
the shirt back of the washboard
musician and carries none
of the heel tap or throaty
moans at issue from a kid
the New Orleans Parish Jail
knocked the wind out of one Sunday.
He stares so far past a crescent
of women bent on the laconic
prospect of dressing him
that he seems to have lost nothing
or sight of the Faubourg Marigny.

Whatever god trips the pilgrims
rounding the cusp of twenty one
from the straight path down Bourbon
stalls too the caning of antiquarians
down the Franco-swamp past of Royal.
Something softer than metal
they want, a smaller bell, smaller
house, something to sting their thighs,
love like it's a poison
to love, a hat with a bigger dent,
body close to bony, a song
like a spell to sit for.

MICHAEL JORDAN

I

Wasn't it the way he stopped dead
at the top of the key
in the thick of a fast break
as physics carried every human
defender past him in a blur—
even our eyes trained on 23
had to back up to center him—
the ball palmed like a yo-yo
in his hand and us agape
at how his knees didn't buckle,
ankle wouldn't snap in its pivot,
how he never even needed arms
to draw circles in the air
for balance like the rest of us
(walking a drunk line
or falling backwards in a pool)—
the trick of his equilibrium
and each motive to score
soothsaid by his tongue
lolling the rim of his lip
like a logo or swished net.

II

Was there ever anyone
so unmoved by gravity,
so happy in this air
between wax and rafter
at the top of the key, this firmament
he ascended for each jump shot and hung
until that cruel gravity
he never endorsed
unwinged his opponent,
dropped him to the earth
like a deviled seraph.
And how he'd unhinge
the lever of his wrist
like he was waving at someone small
or far beneath him, his eyes fixed
on the rim, his tongue, dry as nylon,
readied for the small meal of three,
and how then he'd slake a blessing of sweat
onto the limbs of those fouling below.

CHARLIE CHAN

In the ink of shade cast by a banyan
an actress lies stabbed. It is Waikiki,
and stealing up the beach on the balls
of sandalled feet is Charlie Chan.
He begs your pardon with his eyes peeled
to your tells, and his mind, like an atoll,
gathers clues much as the moon pools salt
water. Perhaps, he thinks, her understudy,
or the ex-director who reminds her
she is past her prime, or maybe the psychic
who peaked behind the curtain of her twenties?

Before the trade winds come to ruffle
the hulk of Diamond Head and purple
the sky above the gaslit waterfront,
he will bow another killer from their
smug party to the rockpile and gauntlet
of old world judgment. He will turn up
Punchbowl Hill with his flivver shuddering
under him, pad by the brick-red bougainvillea
vine to his lanai, the night blotting the white
crest of breakers only his hearing restores,
and only then mourn, only there beside
bamboo and hibiscus with the trades
in his face and eleven children in bed
behind him, only there mourn the dying thing
in him that hardens second sight to a hunch,
the dent of his ancient eyes to lapis,
the placid brow to an avalanche squint
that bears such difficult witness to killing—
a heart that sinks at the unboating of the next liner
from the mainland—the cameras, the flappers,
and once too often the black camel

kneeling at the gate of an aging film star
silenced by talkies and an angry knife.

FATHER BROWN

Always the smallest dot on a village
canvas, this inconspicuous priest,
like the tiny silent Icarus plunging
to the lore of Breughel's netherlandscape.
He is that kind of paradox: the most
skeptical of all believers, the least
assuming of intuitive minds, a face dull
as dumplings, eyes empty as the North Sea.

There is no scandal above his hearing,
no secret he won't guess from a reckless
brogue, a painted hand or bulging sleeve.
He is witness to the impiety
of mirror and light, the perjurous proof
of sound and the betrayal of perspective.
He has seen the world from a hedge ladder
and solved the riddle of locked rooms.
He might be caught cross-legged on the floor
of some parish family's playroom
pinning the florid hat of a wax doll
onto the head of a stuffed monkey,
but he cannot be found in church. Ever.

To understudy his villain he quits
his mind of collars and common sense,
shuts the skylight through which heaven
creeps, then conjures a mind lit by red
light from below, a fire rending rocks
and cleaving the sixth abyss. His voice,
when he speaks, is echo from the vessel
of felon he's become and is, a hollow
where his voice is familiar as trespass,
where he waits to confess his newest self
so we can survive our brief mysteries.

— IV —

SHE'S TURNING THE CORNER ON DITZ

Nothing happens worse than morning.
Or did. Lately her voice wavers like this
between octaves, like the new one she found
while explaining to her lab partner
the strange science by which clownfish
can't have dads. The low voice surprised her
even more than the ease of expression,
and for a second she considered trading in
the twenty minute sting of a butterfly tattoo
for ten more pages of *Madame Bovary*.
It's the sting that moves her through the cusp
of college, that tips the first shot glass
from the second story of the fraternity,
a party beneath her, a guy named Nick
between. It happens as quick as this:
She wakes up with base on again. The boys
turn her around one time too many. Her bob
slows, her squeal tires, and when she wakes one night
to find her friends clutching limes and another
12-pack, her smile dies before it finds her eyes.

IT WAS A KITCHEN TO LIVE IN

The country of her birth only olive
maps have known. Here are lions. Take one,
same colored mane and the breath of thirty days
(he took my brother in his cusp) to the children
of Lilith gathered around the Franklin stove
to blow coals and gossip till dawn.
She swore it was a kitchen to live in—
a window cot for slow bread,
an oil cloth on the butcher's block,
a begonia in a dented kettle.
With fingers knotty as a chicken's neck
she wished the odor of orris root
and damp sheets away one summer,
stubborn as sumac and older, in this kitchen,
beaten into ease by a mother's mother
and her daughter, and all of them
sang when they meant to speak.

JACKDAW SHADE

The sun is too much in Texas
for the traipse of a broken crow.
At noon the pavement burns below
the wing, now snapped, that once was dextrous.
An upcast plea for the shade of trees
or craggy peaks, the three-thirty lean
of a high-rise, a stalled cloud, errant balloon.
Where are they all, he caws,
hopscotching the parking lot
to the belly of a dodge marooned
with a cracked block. The land,
he thinks, flouncing west and shadowless,
is practicing to be a desert. Flat and blanched
by July it is no rival of the sky, pressed
like a child's life to the breast of an angel,
a convex plate to swell the moon's face
in its coming and going. So he raises
the wound like an extra wing, level
to his eye, like he's the lone star vampire
cowering to complain of sun and silver gunfire.
I am the cool moon's feet,
its raven blemish, weeps
the crow. *I pace the rook's file*
with a hoarse and slackjaw cry.

BUTTERFLY BALLOT

The Swallowtails bunch on Florida phlox
like pundits to the flame of argument.
Most prefer thistle to the Shepherd's-needle
parasol so popular among the Sleepy
Orange. They say if you snap off the umbel
at the base and twirl it between your thumb
and birdfinger the arable weed will seem a wheel
whose turning can lull you from the falconress
cries of the media as their grip slips
on the 2000 election. It's an effect that starts
with a butterfly plashing its wings in Palm Beach
and ends with a circus in D.C. The streets
in Palm Beach, to speak of streets, are flat
as the insect grasses of the Loxahatchee
and marked in a language with two wings. Too bad
the anarchy of language is lost on the Cloudless
Sulphur, Crayola lemon wings with spots
like fallen chads beneath. Imagine the cruel child
of Coriolanus punching those spots out with a twig
and you can understand the call to politics.
The first time the world divides is easy—
mother every time. The left breast for the right-
brained, oranges over apples, and anything
but polyester. In the cold war of puberty
we lose faith in things red, in lips and Christmas,
and the sky's godless blue stays a confusion.
Maybe we take donkeys over elephants
but it's less a question of smell than sound.
But why break a Monarch on a wheel,
or pin one to a cork board with the pale fire
of a novelist. If we lay the ballot down
with the gentler tuck of a mother

we see its thorax is a map of bad
choices: one flits down an oil-slick back
road; the other turns left in right angles,
so that even his circling is square.

.

A FAULT FOR APPLAUSE

One clap from the Classics chair
and a bony oak doffs a false crown
of grackles into an early March mist.

Since he no longer recalls the beach
of his childhood, this flush of blackbirds
into a north Texas dusk sounds more like

the spirant gust of flame from his gas range.
He calls nature a brittle nostalgia now.
He looks up for rain or bits of bird

once they touch him. And he claps
like a faltering god, not to stop
the cawing, not to cause the birds

purfled on the oak's rim to lift
enormous into the twilit sky. (His hands
for emphases were wings once).

He claps instead for that brief hush
between, when before rising
the grackles gasp at his clapping.

It's a quiet he knows, like the silence
of finals, or the hush of distrust at a too-
simple question, when chin

to chest his students feather
their memories, and youth lifts
its fluttering hand to answer.

MERCURY

Hatters went mad to stroke the brims
of derbies and bowlers with it,
the riddle of their nervous jerks
and rude remarks no long wonder,

but think of the tongue that licks
the mail closed but forks its course—up
to the core to which most blood boils,
slow as hot August, some things red

bent on levitation. The smallest planet
is sun-bent, rises like quicksilver
to the hammer of circus strongmen,
their zeal a climbing fever,

or falls like poison from a quill
onto the page of a suicide,
the soul a broken diode, sin
lyric. With catgut strung across

a tortoise husk, he strums a hymn
to suture wounds made of errancy
and loss, to guard both thief and merchant,
to walk smooth-shod and swiftly

into sleep, where gods and mortals
meet in a cloverleaf of speech,
and he still hawks poems like news,
as welcome in heaven as in hell.

DR. EMERITUS SPEAKS
AT THE DEPARTMENT MEETING

What I want to say, and I don't precisely know
what the other full professors, though
I have spoken to Portia, have heard
about the third, I believe it was the third,
proposal you mention in last week's
minutes, which I, a grammarian, though a meek
one, would like to friendlily—a word,
you know—amend; at any rate, this third,
or was it fourth, item is, if I understand
it correctly, somewhat quixotic and
gratuitously long-winded, don't you think,
at least in the manner of its articulation
by our junior colleague Mister Maeterlinck—
it is Mister, is it not?—and runs the risk
of transgressing the letter of our, tsk tsk,
bylaws, the very document that Donald
and I, hello Donald, worked to chisel
from its previous incarnation by the (cough)
New Critics that gorged at the trough
of any poet's whim, to its present
Galatea, stripping, as we did, the prolix
robes from her milky limbs, the linoleum
adjectives from the foundational verbs
about her lovely feet, and laying before
you the beauty you are about to wave away
with the air of someone tossing a salad.

ALIEN ABDUCTION

It must be a rupture like waking,
all that light, telepathy and dental work,
and like the sever in the sylvan groove
that secrets bad sex and calculus
you bury it, deeper than infancy,
deeper even than the memoir
closed by birth, each leaf a little mattress
beneath which the memory sits
like a shelled and irksome legume
not even the fussiest princess senses.

But in the face of every fetus
is an alien: the disproportionate
head, blunted and sexless, eyes
like raindrops, sleepy and dark.

If it was flesh that muffled the sound
of your mother's voice,
you might swear all talk was telepathy.
If born into a hospital fluorescence,
you might recall a blinding light,
what Saul saw and called God.

Or say your head pushed out ahead
of your shrunken and colored self,
the pressure it suffers might seem
a vice for curious surgery. Torn

from the warm swamp of her womb
against your living will, you'd remember
a struggle, like abduction, a gallery
of eyes and the naked sensation
of being watched, for the first time.

I'M NOT UP SO MUCH AS YOU ARE DOWN

Off the sidewalks here cornsnow
bounces like packing peanuts fallen
to the prodigious feet of mice.
Scratch prodigious. The cool kids
ditch school and stomp on the corners
like their feet are on fire. Even the dogs
blow smoke in the streets. Today,
a girl with China white skin
said drop the accent or drop your pants,
so I thought of you. Two step,
cornbread, your polysyllabic damns.
Always more of a drawl than a twang.

EL NIÑO

I used to take the weather personally.
I still overreact to harbor waves
and thunderheads, to the way steam
lifting from summer asphalt can gauze

the splayed sunlight and harlequin rainbow.
Even the moon glow of midnight snow
drives me to distraction, or dawn,
to a chant for the maxims of daylight,

sunk to my elbow in a dirty syringe.
I don't expect much, but I'd like once
to be left alone with the hailstones
that caused an industry in car repair.

I don't doubt the conspiracy of thunder
our fathers, not in heaven, rented from the sky
to grumble uninterrupted, but my dad's no god,
sun or otherwise, and he'd never give me the keys

to drive day's chariot around the bumpy
universe. And this boy, el niño, this child
of the sun blowing a chaos of weather
onto the belly of a sagging superpower,

I've never met him. Though I know what it means
to shrink from a sun's ridiculous wattage,
night is not long enough for both sleep
and heroin. But I'd never say so—

not to the child coughing twisters into the gulf,
or the man bent over his ulcer and a seismic chart,
not to anyone who'd gauge the quaking
or breaking of the earth by its faults.

HEROIN

Un punto solo me maggior letargo
  che venticinque secoli a la'mpresa
  che fe' Nettuno ammirar l'ombra d'Argo

        Paradiso 33

I

It's not sleep exactly, or mandragora,
no nap off the path to Oz,
neither is it a stall-tactic snack
for the homecoming hero,
too contentedly slow in return.

More than a dalliance in flowers,
its gentle smell greets you like age:
a full stomach, the roving itch,
a penchant for moon-dull light.

You think you want both the shelter of bark
and the heart to beat beneath the bark,
where the plural nerves of laurel, like Daphne,
weep onto the shoulder of a river.

For her only the deepest wood would do,
her fear drawn from a fat child's quiver.
When love is a wound, we drug it.

II

Spoon. You number it second of the shapes
your mouth memorizes as a child.
Your only skin is silence then,
your only silence sleep. Now each one
in the silverware drawer rests on a crescent
blackened by flame, the silver charred
and darkness spreading like the dilated
pupil of a woman sick with morning,
the insolent light flooding its nerves. Call it
a decanter of ails to travel you, mother's
coaxing arm, the bed of breakfast.
In it you boil out the cut, the dirt,
till it's pure junk and a curious yellow
gold. Empty you find a concave face in it,
brittle as silver, shallow and stainless as steel.

III

Plunge is some of it, the taste of blood
sublingual, the rush of warmth
that laps through your heart till a pulse
of pleasure deepens to a nod.
You want both the armor of junk
and your heart to beat beneath.

So quick is its spell that you forget
to pull out the syringe sometimes,
and it bobs at the bend in your elbow
like the prick on a fickle boy,
or the question he saves for a certain
girl, like: Why have you driven
through my heart? Make that what.

IV

You always wake before the needle pricks
the vein, almost always before you suck
the tar through the balled cotton you mop
the bowl of a spoon with, careful not to dull
your works. Before the browned, soggy ball dries
and whitens as you pull the plunger up.

The bulk of the plot is mostly chase,
what with sanguine faith you call score.
In each dream there are friends to ditch,
family to rob, women to make wait and betray
as waking turns on you—when the dream, dope,
the flu in your body and every poem you write
to kill it, withdraws. When shaking and awake
you beg for the laurel's cloak
and your heart to slow beneath.

THE HAND OF BEATRICE

Is not so much methadone as the girl
at the gate of his maze with a thread
to knot the needle of his twenties
and draw out the life heroin buried.
She likes pretty cakes. Likes murders
solved. If you listen close you can hear
the diphthong in the middle of her cat
Toby as she calls him back from Georgia.

She is pinkest where she opens—
like the polished mouth of an empty conch,
a Triton's trumpet, the ocean's ear.
And she opens like an ear to a question
or like a question to the sea's
redundant thunder and spray.

All that moss and gothic gasping,
she can't help it if she pushes the O
out of her mouth like it's a dirndl. As for him,
he can't help everything and his arms
if they fly from their sides when he sees her
and reaches for the tenth of ten heavens.

.

DEL SOL PRESS, based out of Washington, D.C., publishes exemplary and edgy fiction, poetry, and nonfiction (mostly contemporary, with the occasional reprint). Founded in 2002, the press sponsors two annual competitions:

THE DEL SOL PRESS POETRY PRIZE is a yearly book-length competition with a January deadline for an unpublished book of poems. The judge for 2003 was Lucie Brock-Broido, and the contest winner was Austin Hummell's *Poppy*.

THE ROBERT OLEN BUTLER FICTION PRIZE is awarded for the best short story, published or unpublished. The deadline is in November of each year.

Full guidelines and more information are available on the website:

http://webdelsol.com/DelSolPress

AUSTIN HUMMELL's first book, *The Fugitive Kind,* was a winner of the Contemporary Poetry Series Competition and was published by the University of Georgia Press. He teaches at Northern Michigan University and is poetry editor of *Passages North.*

Printed in the United States
23599LVS00007B/86